WHEN YOU PRAY

MATTHEW K. THOMPSON

MATTHEW K. THOMPSON

Copyright © 2021 Matthew K. Thompson

TABLE OF CONTENTS

DEDICATION

To my love, my wife, my dream, my queen. He who finds a wife finds a good thing and obtains favor from the Lord. Thank you, Mona, for loving me, believing in me and being my favor. You are my everything.

WHEN YOU PRAY

Jesus is having a conversation with the Disciples in Matthew 6:5 and he says to them, "When you PRAY..." These incredible words from Jesus have created a cry in my heart and a determination in my spirit to live a life of prayer. In this text, Jesus is making an assumption that we; His disciples, His children, His followers, have uncovered the power, importance and necessity of Prayer. I have grown to depend upon my time of prayer with my Heavenly Father. When you PRAY, mountains move. When you PRAY, demons tremble. When you PRAY, all of Heaven stands at attention to hear your worship, to attend to your concerns, to open the windows of Heaven, to dispatch angels from Heaven to guard you and your children, your church, your city, your region, your nation, and our world. I am praying and believing that as you pray these prophetic prayers with me, you will believe that all of Heaven will stand at attention to hear your cries, the petitions from your heart, and you will believe with me that your prayers will garner Heaven's attention. Let us PRAY...

Our Father in Heaven

hallowed be Your name,

Your kingdom come,

Your will be done,

on earth as it is in Heaven.

Give us today our daily bread.

And forgive us our debts,

as we also have forgiven our debtors.

And lead us not into temptation,

but deliver us from the evil one.

For Thine is the kingdom and the power

and the glory, forever. (Matthew 6:9-13)

James 4:7

Submit yourselves, then, to God. Resist the devil, and he will flee from you. (NIV)

Today we are withholding nothing from our God. What are you surrendering to the Lord today? Write below.

SURRENDER

Today, all of Heaven stands at attention to hear the cries of my heart. I am nothing without You, You are the air that I breathe, You are the song that I sing. I am breathing the breath that You gave me to breathe to worship You, to adore You, to lift up Your name high above the Heavens. Your name is the only name that is worthy of my praise, and with my very last breath I will declare of Your mighty acts of grace and mercy that You have lavished upon me. Today, I want You to know that I don't praise You or pray to You because of all that You have done for me. I lift my hands, I lift my voice, I am determined to live a life of surrender just because of who You are, and because of who You are, I give You my life. You can use all of me. In Jesus' name. Amen.

1 Thessalonians 5:18

Give thanks in all circumstances; for this is God's will for you in Christ Jesus. (NIV)

List 15 things that you are thankful for today.

1.

2.

3.

4.

5.

6.

7.

8.

9.

10.

11.

12.

13.

14.

15.

THANKSGIVING

Today, all of Heaven stands at attention to hear the cries of my heart. Lord, I thank You that I am breathing the breath that You blessed me to breathe. I thank You that I have the activity of my limbs. When my feet hit the floor this morning, I lifted my hands and my heart in total praise to You for all that You have done, for all that You are doing, for the things to come, and all the blessings that are on the way. With the fruit of my lips, I give You the praise and adoration unto Your name. You are great and You do miracles so great. I am thankful for the miracle of life, and today, I pause to thank you for my life. In Jesus' name. Amen.

Psalm 107:1

Give thanks to the Lord, for he is good; his love endures forever. (NIV)

Today, take some time to write down your testimony. What has the Lord done in your life? Where has he taken you from? What miracles have you experienced? Write below.

GRATEFULNESS

Today, all of Heaven stands at attention to hear the cries of my heart. Before I ask You for anything I want to thank You for everything, and for all that You have done for me. If I had ten thousand tongues, it would not be enough to thank you for all that You have done for me. Thank You for Your goodness, Your mercy, and Your grace that You have poured upon my life. When I was in the darkest period in my life, You revealed Yourself to me and I am forever grateful. Today, I just wanted You to know that if You never did another thing for me, You have done enough. Thank you. Thank you. Thank you, Jesus.

Psalm 27:14

Wait for the Lord; be strong and take heart and wait for the Lord. (NIV)

Today, spend some time waiting on the Lord in prayer. Clear your mind and stay silent. Ask the Lord to speak to you. What is He saying? Write below.

WAITING

Today, all of Heaven stands at attention to hear the cries of my heart. Isaiah 40:31 says, "They that wait on the Lord, shall renew their strength, they shall mount up on wings like an eagle; they shall run and not grow weary, they shall walk and not faint." Father, I am grateful for the power of waiting in Your presence. In Your presence there is peace, in Your presence there is hope, in Your presence there is joy, in Your presence there is revelation, in Your presence there is freedom, in Your presence there is strength. I need Your supernatural strength today to withstand the winds of life. I am strong because of You. I have made it this far because of You. I am still standing because of You. I am still in my right mind because of You. I recognize the importance of waiting for You and waiting in Your presence for the strength that I need for today, tomorrow and my future. In Jesus' name. Amen.

Psalm 91:2

I will say of the Lord, "He is my refuge and my fortress, my God, in whom I trust." (NIV)

Why do you trust the Lord? Every now and then we all need a reminder of why we trust Jesus. Tell the Lord why you trust Him. Write below.

FAITHFULNESS

Today, all of Heaven stands at attention to hear the cries of my heart. In the midst of the ever-changing landscape of this world, I am so blessed that I can trust in a never changing God. You love me with an everlasting, unconditional love. Even as the world may change, and things may shift, and the storms of life are raging; You are and have always been the same yesterday, today, and forever. On Christ the solid rock I stand, all other ground is sinking sand. I thank You for being my firm foundation, my solid rock, my hiding place and my refuge. I know that I can depend on You. Thank You for being my anchor. In Jesus' name. Amen.

Isaiah 60:1

Arise, shine, for your light has come, and the glory of the Lord rises upon you. (NIV)

Today we are declaring God's glory in our lives. Choose five areas in your life where you want God's glory to shine.

1.

2.

3.

4.

5.

GLORY

Today, all of Heaven stands at attention to hear the cries of my heart. I am desperate. I am desperate for Your Glory to be revealed in my life. I have been praying for years that the knowledge of the Glory of the Lord will cover the earth like the waters cover the seas. I am desperate for Your Glory to be revealed in my life, my home, my business, my school, my city, my region, my nation, our world. If it's a matter of hunger or of desperation, Lord, I want You to know that whatever You require of me, here I am. Today, I am determined to be desperately in the passionate pursuit of Your presence, and the fulfillment of Your Glory in every area of my life, in the name of Jesus Christ. Amen.

Romans 8:28

And we know that in all things God works for the good of those who love him, who have been called according to his purpose. (NIV)

Today we are declaring that all things are working together for our good. As you pray, spend some time listening to God's voice. What is the Lord saying? Write below.

PURPOSE

Today, all of Heaven stands at attention to hear the cries of my heart. In a world full of confusion and false realities, there is a clarion call for the people of God to stand and call on the name of the Lord! May the purpose of God be made known to me today, oh great Jehovah. You said in Jeremiah 29:11, "For I know the plans I have for you," declares the Lord, "plans to prosper you and not to harm you, plans to give you hope and a future." Father, I thank You today that my purpose is not hidden from me. Today, I ask You for a clear revelation and understanding of my purpose. Show me a sign today, remind me of a childhood memory that will lead me on a journey, a discovery of the God-given destiny for my life. I recognize how much I need Your guidance, Your direction, Your instruction, especially in understanding and pursuing my purpose. In Jesus' name, reveal Yourself to me, so that I may walk in the blessing and provision of purpose. Amen.

Jeremiah 33:6

Nevertheless, I will bring health and healing to it; I will heal my people and will let them enjoy abundant peace and security. (NIV)

Today we are declaring God's healing over our community. List 3 things that you want the Lord to heal your community from.

1.

2.

3.

HEALING (LAND)

Today, all of Heaven stands at attention to hear the cries of my heart. You said in 2 Chronicles 7:14, "if My people who are called by My name would humble themselves and pray and seek..." Today, we humble ourselves and pray, and we seek Your face. We are the generations that will seek Your face. It's not that we don't need Your hand to move, but we humble ourselves and are determined to seek Your face. You said You would hear from Heaven, forgive our sins and heal our land. Heal our land from violence. Heal our land from division. Heal our land from perversion. Heal our land from legalism. Heal our land from racism and injustice. Heal our land from the plague of unbelief, that would blind us from seeing the truth of Your goodness and grace. In the mighty, matchless name of Jesus Christ. Amen.

John 4:14

But whoever drinks the water I give them will never thirst. Indeed, the water I give them will become in them a spring of water welling up to eternal life. (NIV)

God's grace has been covering us before we entered our mothers' womb. Can you remember a time when God's grace rescued you? Write it down as a sign of your testimony.

GRACE

Today, all of Heaven stands at attention to hear the cries of my heart. In a dry and desolate land, I long for the experience of living water, a water that will quench my thirst. I have tried before to rely on other things, or people, or substances to meet a need that I now understand can only be met with Your grace, Your amazing grace. The water of Your grace has covered my life and has restored my soul in seasons of drought, in moments of despair. Thank You, Jesus, for being patient with me. When I was searching You waited on me, and I am forever grateful. And now that I have the living water, the only water, the refreshing water of Your word, I am determined to share this water that will never run dry. Today, I pray: make me a conduit of Your living water, to offer hope, life, and renewal to a dry and desert land. In Jesus' name. Amen.

John 14:27

Peace I leave with you; my peace I give you. I do not give to you as the world gives. Do not let your hearts be troubled and do not be afraid. (NIV)

Are there any parts of your life that don't appear peaceful? Take some time to be specific and declare peace over those situations and circumstances. Write below.

PEACE

Today, all of Heaven stands at attention to hear the cries of my heart. Lord, I thank You for being my Jehovah Shalom. You are my peace. You are my peace in the midst of the storm. I have gone through several storms in my life, and I thank You for being with me. You have always been near me, with me, and for me. I know that if God be for me, who can be against me? So today, I am grateful that in the complexities of life's ever-changing landscape, Your peace has calmed the storms in my life. You said in Your word that You will keep me in perfect peace, if I keep my mind stayed upon You. (Isaiah 26:3) I am determined to keep my mind stayed on You, and I am confident that the peace that surpasses all understanding will guard my heart and my mind in Christ Jesus.

Hebrews 12:1-3

Therefore, since we are surrounded by such a great cloud of witnesses, let us throw off everything that hinders and the sin that so easily entangles. And let us run with perseverance the race marked out for us, fixing our eyes on Jesus, the pioneer and perfecter of faith. For the joy set before him he endured the cross, scorning its shame, and sat down at the right hand of the throne of God. Consider him who endured such opposition from sinners, so that you will not grow weary and lose heart.

As you pray for endurance, it is important to know the goal and destination. Where is the Lord taking you? In 5 years, in 10 years, in 20 years? Take some time to write down your goals and aspirations.

ENDURANCE

Today, all of Heaven stands at attention to hear the cries of my heart. Lord, I need Your endurance. You said in Your word, that we should not grow weary in doing well, but in due season, we will reap a harvest, if we do not faint, if we do not give up. (Galatians 6:9) Today, I am asking for supernatural endurance to withstand the challenges and trappings of this world that have tried, unsuccessfully, to get me to give up and throw in the towel. I will not give up. I will not lose heart. I will not become discouraged. Today is the day that I take control over my confession, and I declare that no matter what comes my way, I will not grow weary, I will stand in the confidence that You have given to me in Jesus' name. Amen.

Matthew 6:25-26

Therefore I tell you, do not worry about your life, what you will eat or drink; or about your body, what you will wear. Is not life more than food, and the body more than clothes? Look at the birds of the air; they do not sow or reap or store away in barns, and yet your heavenly Father feeds them. Are you not much more valuable than they?

Today as you endeavor to trust in the Lord, what are you placing in his hands? What are you letting go of? Take some time to write it down and let God have his way.

BURDEN

Today, all of Heaven stands at attention to hear the cries of my heart. Today is a very challenging day for me. I am feeling the weight of grief and sadness. You said in 1 Peter 5:7, "Cast all your cares upon him, for He cares for you." So, even in the midst of sadness and grief, I release the burden of carrying something that I was never designed to carry. You said in Your word in Matthew 11:30, "For My yoke is easy and My burden is light." In times past, I tried to do everything on my own and it never worked. I have decided to take my hands off the wheel, and trust You with this burden that I am carrying. I am determined to leave this here in your hands because You are a specialist in dealing with pain and grief and sadness. Today I trust You with the affairs of this life and I am determined to walk in your freedom forever. In Jesus' name. Amen.

Proverbs 3:13-18

Blessed are those who find wisdom,

    those who gain understanding,

for she is more profitable than silver

    and yields better returns than gold.

She is more precious than rubies;

    nothing you desire can compare with her

Long life is in her right hand;

    in her left hand are riches and honor.

Her ways are pleasant ways,

    and all her paths are peace.

She is a tree of life to those who take hold of her;

    those who hold her fast will be blessed. (NIV)

What decisions or circumstances on which do you need God's wisdom? Take some time and write them down. After you have written them down, pray on each one and ask the Lord for his wisdom.

WISDOM

Today, all of Heaven stands at attention to hear the cries of my heart. The Bible states that if any man lacks wisdom, and he asks for it, it will be given freely to him. Today, I desire to walk in the wisdom of God. Give me wisdom to navigate this day. Give me wisdom to hear and understand the voice of God this day. Grant me wisdom to discern the situations that are presented to me today. Grant me the wisdom to walk in the abundance that You have promised me. In Jesus' name. Amen.

Romans 5:9

Since we have now been justified by his blood, how much more shall we be saved from God's wrath through him! (NIV)

You are covered under the blood of Jesus Christ. Make a list of all the things you are declaring the blood of Jesus over today.

1.

2.

3.

4.

5.

6.

7.

8.

9.

10.

11.

12.

RIGHTEOUSNESS

Today, all of Heaven stands at attention to hear the cries of my heart. Thank You for being my Jehovah Tsidkenu, You are my righteousness. Today, I can boldly stand in right standing with You, not because I am perfect, but because I have surrendered to Your word, Your will, and Your way for my life. I am covered by the shed blood of Jesus Christ, and I thank You that the blood still works. It reaches the highest mountain and it flows to the lowest valley. The blood that gives me strength from day to day, week to week, month to month, year to year, decade to decade, generation to generation, it will never lose its power! The blood still works, and I am under the shed blood of Jesus Christ. Therefore, I am standing in the righteousness that Your blood has provided for me. In Jesus' name. Amen.

Joel 2:25-26

I will repay you for the years the locusts have eaten—

    the great locust and the young locust,

    the other locusts and the locust swarm—

my great army that I sent among you.

You will have plenty to eat, until you are full,

    and you will praise the name of the Lord your God,

    who has worked wonders for you;

never again will my people be shamed. (NIV)

List 3 things the enemy has stolen from you? After you have listed them, take some time to declare God's restoration over your life. When He restores those things, come back to this page to see God's faithfulness.

   1.

   2.

   3.

SOUL RESTORATION

Today, all of Heaven stands at attention to hear the cries of my heart. I thank You for being my Jehovah Rohi, You are my Shepherd. Today, I determine that I shall not be in want because You are all that I need. You make me lie down in green pastures, You lead me beside quiet waters, and You restore my soul! Thank You, Jesus, for soul restoration. The trappings of the world have infected my soul, but You are my Jehovah Rohi. You have restored my soul, You are watching over my soul, and when I need restoration You are there to work on me. Thank You for loving me through the pain, and thank You for insulating my soul. In Jesus' name. Amen.

Jeremiah 17:14

Heal me, Lord, and I will be healed; save me and I will be saved, for you are the one I praise. (NIV)

Today we are declaring that we are healed! What is the Lord healing you from today? Write below.

HEALING (BODY)

Today, all of Heaven stands at attention to hear the cries of my heart. Thank You for being my Jehovah Rapha. I declare that sickness cannot dwell in my body. I believe that the number of my days, my God will fulfill. In Isaiah 53 You said, "He was wounded for our transgressions, He was crushed for our iniquities; the punishment that brought us peace was upon Him, and by His stripes we are healed." Today, I am praying that Jehovah Rapha, the healing nature and nurturing of God will rest upon my body. I cancel the assignment of every sickness, every infirmity, every disease. I declare and proclaim today, that because of the shed blood of Jesus, and the stripes that He took on my behalf, I am healed, I am free, and I am walking in the grace of the miraculous. In Jesus' name. Amen.

Matthew 7:7

Ask and it will be given to you; seek and you will find; knock and the door will be opened to you. (NIV)

Today the Lord wants to hear the desires of your heart. As you pray, write down what it is you want. Be open and honest, hold nothing back, your Father is listening.

SEEKING

Today, all of Heaven stands at attention to hear the cries of my heart. I have heard it said that, "he who hungers and thirsts after righteousness shall be filled," (Matthew 5:6) filled with the full measure of God. Today, Jesus, I want You to know that I want everything that You have for me. If I have done something to prevent the full measure, search me, oh Great Jehovah. Whatever I need to do to walk in the full measure of Your glory, Your favor, Your power in my life, that is what I desire. You said in Jeremiah 29, that I will find You, if I search for You with all my heart. I am searching, I am knocking, I am willing to be all that You have called me to be. I am ready for the full measure of Your favor to rest upon me this day, in the name of the Lord Jesus Christ. Amen.

2 Corinthians 9:10

Now he who supplies seed to the sower and bread for food will also supply and increase your store of seed and will enlarge the harvest of your righteousness. (NIV)

More is on the way! Today, take some time to prepare for the harvest. How are you preparing for more? What will you do with the "more" that God is sending you? Take some time to write down a plan of action.

HARVEST

Today, all of Heaven stands at attention to hear the cries of my heart. Today, I can admit that I am tired and there are times that I grow weary, but I am reminded that I should not grow weary in doing well, for in due season, I will reap a harvest if I do not faint. I have decided that I will not faint, I will not give up, I will not give in. Therefore, I declare my harvest is coming, my abundance is here. I am a breakthrough professional and what may seem impossible with man, is completely possible with the King of Kings who is on my side. Today, I stand in the corridors of faith and declare my harvest is coming. I declare doors are open, I declare blessings are flowing, I declare victory today is mine. In Jesus' name. Amen.

Isaiah 41:10

So do not fear, for I am with you; do not be dismayed, for I am your God. I will strengthen you and help you; I will uphold you with my righteous right hand. (NIV)

Today we are choosing faith over fear! What do you have faith for in this season of your life? Write below.

FEAR

Today, all of Heaven stands at attention to hear the cries of my heart. Hear my cry, oh God, attend unto my prayers. From the ends of the earth will I cry unto Thee. When my heart is overwhelmed, lead me to the rock that is higher than I. We find ourselves at a crossroads today. Will we choose faith or will we choose fear? The fear of the Lord is the beginning of wisdom, and knowledge of the Holy One is understanding. For through You, our days will be many and years will be added to our lives. (Proverbs 9:10-11) Today, we have a healthy fear of You, our King, and that fear will lead us to a place full of wisdom; wisdom that can only come from the throne room of God. Today I choose wisdom, I choose faith, and I will walk in the abundance of wisdom. In Jesus' name. Amen.

Philippians 4:19

And my God will meet all your needs according to the riches of his glory in Christ Jesus. (NIV)

Our God always provides. Can you think of a time when you were in need and God provided exactly what you needed? Take some time to write it down, as a reminder of God's faithfulness.

PROVISION

Today, all of Heaven stands at attention to hear the cries of my heart. I thank You for being my Jehovah Jireh, You are my provider. When I look back over my life I recognize that I never would have made it, if it had not been for Your provision. You have always provided a way for me; a way of salvation, a way of forgiveness, a way of prosperity, a way of healing, a way of peace, a way of freedom, a way of deliverance. You are my waymaker. You are more than enough for me. Today I acknowledge You as the source of my strength, I acknowledge You as my rock, I acknowledge You as my refuge, I acknowledge You as my provider. And if You never do another thing for me, You have done more than enough. You are my Jehovah Jireh. In Jesus' name. Amen

James 5:16

Therefore confess your sins to each other and pray for each other so that you may be healed. The prayer of a righteous person is powerful and effective. (NIV)

The Lord is calling for us to be intercessors. Make a list of some things God is asking you to intercede for in prayer.

1.

2.

3.

4.

5.

6.

7.

8.

9.

10.

INTERCESSION

Today, all of Heaven stands at attention to hear the cries of my heart. In a world that is longing and searching for a savior, I am blessed beyond words to know that my Redeemer lives and He is making intercession for me. Thank you, Jesus, for interceding for me. I recognize that I am still standing because of Your goodness, Your mercy, Your grace, and Your intercession. The enemy will not sift me as wheat because You have prayed for me, my faith is rising, and I am getting stronger. As I grow in my strength, Lord, I am asking that You would make me an intercessor. Make me an intercessor that I may stand in the gap for the needs of my family, my church, and my community. You said in Ezekiel 22:30, "I searched for someone among them who would build up the wall and stand before me in the gap on behalf of the land so I would not destroy it, but I found no one." Here I am Lord, standing in a place of expectation and intercession. You can use me. In Jesus' name. Amen.

Romans 5:8

But God demonstrates his own love for us in this: While we were still sinners, Christ died for us. (NIV)

Today write your own love letter to Jesus. Let Him know why you love Him and how you plan on loving Him for the rest of your life. Write below.

LOVE

Today, all of Heaven stands at attention to hear the cries of my heart. I am determined to assume the posture of surrender. I surrender everything, everything that I have, withholding nothing. Forgive me for trying to bargain with You, oh great Jehovah, You have been so patient with me. I know I don't deserve it, but still You have waited for me and pursued me. You are the God of the second chance, thank You for all the chances that You have bestowed upon me. Today, my eyes are open to the truth and I promise to serve You with all that is within me, until my very last breath. You deserve all of me because You have sacrificed all of You. You first loved me. Thank you, Jesus, for Your sacrifice. Thank you, Jesus, for Your persistent and passionate pursuit of Your purpose, to shed Your blood so that I may live a life of passion, provision and purpose. Today, I give You all of me, in the mighty name of Jesus Christ. Amen.

Psalm 138:7

Though I walk in the midst of trouble,

   you preserve my life.

You stretch out your hand against the anger of my foes;

   with your right hand you save me. (NIV)

God will always protect you. Can you think of a time God has protected you from danger? Write it down as a reminder, if he did it before he can do it again!

PROTECTION

Today, all of Heaven stands at attention to hear the cries of my heart. I have come to know You in a very real way. There have been times in my life where my faith was weak and there were questions I had concerning my future. I can honestly say that I have asked the question, "is God punishing me for a mistake that I made?" As I have matured in my faith and in my walk with You, I have come to know You as my savior, my deliverer, my doctor, my counselor, my present help in the time of trouble. When I look back over the course of my life I recognize that, even in those questioning seasons, Your hand was always on me, Your presence was always protecting me. And now, I can thank You for the storm and give You praise for carrying me through and keeping me in the shadows. You said in Your word that You would never leave me nor forsake me. Thank You, Jesus, for protecting me from me, and for allowing me to experience the blessings and peace that comes with Your protection. In Jesus' name. Amen

Psalm 91:1-2

Whoever dwells in the shelter of the Most High

will rest in the shadow of the Almighty.

I will say of the Lord, "He is my refuge and my fortress,

my God, in whom I trust." (NIV)

God is calling us to dwell in His presence today. As you dwell and rest in Him, how do you feel? Write down the effect of His presence in your heart, mind and soul.

DWELL

Today, all of Heaven stands at attention to hear the cries of my heart. How lovely is Your dwelling place, oh great Jehovah. When I think about the works of Your hands and the majesty and splendor of Your name, I am overwhelmed with Your love for me. I long to dwell in Your tent and I desire to be found in Your presence day to day, to behold Your beauty and be in a place where I feel the safety of Your wings. Today, I make the decision to dwell in Your presence, to prioritize Your presence, and to find the peace within Your presence that will cause my life to sing a song of adoration to Your name. In Jesus' name. Amen

Mark 11:24

Therefore I tell you, whatever you ask for in prayer, believe that you have received it, and it will be yours. (NIV)

What are you asking the Lord for in prayer today? Make a list, and believe that you have received it.

1.

2.

3.

4.

5.

6.

7.

8.

9.

10.

OPEN DOORS

Today, all of Heaven stands at attention to hear the cries of my heart. You said in Matthew 7:7, "ask and it shall be given, seek and you will find, knock and the door will be opened to you." Father, here I am asking for the windows of Heaven to be opened over my life. Here I am seeking Your face because I recognize that if I am in Your presence, I will experience the abundance of an open Heaven. Here I am knocking on the door and I believe with all my heart that every door, every opportunity that You have for me, will be opened. I thank You for opening doors. I have now come to understand the protection in the closed door. Your ways are higher than mine and Your plan for my life is beyond my comprehension. I surrender my will and I am determined to trust Your ways so that the blessings of Your promise will be added to every area of my life. In Jesus' name. Amen.

Proverbs 3:5-6

Trust in the Lord with all your heart

   and lean not on your own understanding;

in all your ways submit to him,

   and he will make your paths straight. (NIV)

The Lord is directing your path. Take some time to pray and listen to the voice of God. Where is He telling you to go? What direction is He giving you? Write below.

DIRECTION

Today, all of Heaven stands at attention to hear the cries of my heart. You said in Proverbs 3:5-6 to "trust in the Lord with all your heart and lean not on your own understanding, but in all your ways acknowledge Him and He will direct your paths." I acknowledge Your presence in my life. I am fully aware of the reality that I am nothing without You. It is in You that I live and move and have my being. (Acts 17:28) Thank You for saving me and for rescuing me from myself and the trappings of this world, that attempted to destroy my life and testimony. I have arrived at this place of surrender and revelation of Your unique design for my life, and I am determined to trust in You fully. I will put my full weight on you today! Thank You for education and knowledge and understanding. Today, I acknowledge You as the source of my strength, the source of my hope and I know without a shadow of a doubt that You are directing my paths in the name of the Lord Jesus Christ. In Jesus' name. Amen.

Isaiah 43:19

See, I am doing a new thing!

Now it springs up; do you not perceive it?

I am making a way in the wilderness

and streams in the wasteland. (NIV)

You are stepping into the new! What are you leaving behind? Make a list of the things you are leaving behind today.

1.

2.

3.

4.

5.

6.

7.

8.

9.

10.

11.

12.

RENEWAL

Today, all of Heaven stands at attention to hear the cries of my heart. 2 Corinthians 5:17 states, "if any man be in Christ, he is a new creation, the old man is gone and behold all things have become new." Yesterday is gone and today is a new day, a new beginning, and new beginnings require new decisions. Today, I decide to begin again. Old ways, old thoughts, old habits -- the old is gone and I am determined to walk in the blessings of becoming a new creation. Thank You, Jesus, for insulating me and protecting me from the traps of the enemy. I am still alive, I am still in my right mind and I have lived long enough to hear, respond, believe and walk in the abundance of becoming a new creation. In Jesus' name. Amen.

Proverbs 18:21

Death and life are in the power of the tongue. (NKJV)

Today we are commanding our atmospheres to shift! What is God shifting around you today? Declare it below.

ATMOSPHERE SHIFT

Today, all of Heaven stands at attention to hear the cries of my heart. The Bible says in Acts 16:25, "About midnight Paul and Silas were praying and singing hymns to God, and the other prisoners were listening to them. Suddenly there was such a violent earthquake that the foundations of the prison were shaken..." Today I am praying for an atmosphere shifting anointing to rest upon my life, rest upon my home, rest upon my church, rest upon my city, rest upon my region, rest upon our nation, rest upon our world! Lord, send a sudden shaking that will shift our perspectives so we can see You again. Open the eyes of our heart so we can see You. Send a shaking in our lives that will allow us to see the world the way You see it. Help us to see ourselves the way You see us. Help us to see children the way You see them. Help us to see our spouses the way You see them. Help us to see our church the way You see Your church. Open the prison doors and shift the atmosphere in our lives so that we can share the Good News of Jesus Christ. Amen.

Romans 10:9

If you declare with your mouth, "Jesus is Lord," and believe in your heart that God raised him from the dead, you will be saved. (NIV)

Who are you praying into salvation? Write their names below and commit to praying for them daily.

1.

2.

3.

4.

5.

6.

7.

8.

9.

10.

SALVATION

Today, all of Heaven stands at attention to hear the cries of my heart. You said in 2 Corinthians 4:4, "The god of this age has blinded the minds of unbelievers, so that they cannot see the light of the gospel that displays the glory of Christ, who is the image of God." Today, great Jehovah I am praying that You will save _____! I am asking You to break every generational curse, every demonic hindrance, every lie from the pit of hell that has been unleashed to attack and derail _____ from walking in their prophetic destiny. I break the hold of the enemy off of their lives now! Every form of addiction, manipulation and perversion is crushed now, under the weight and glory of the name of Jesus. Every knee will bow and every tongue will confess that Jesus is Lord. (Philippians 2:10-11) Today I pray that _____ will receive Your goodness, Your mercy, Your grace and that every form of blindness is broken off of their lives now, In Jesus Name we pray. Amen.

Isaiah 54:13

All your children will be taught by the Lord, and great will be their peace. (NIV)

What are you declaring over your children today? Take some time to write it down.

CHILDREN

Today, all of Heaven stands at attention to hear the cries of my Heart. The Bible says in Psalm 127:3, "Children are a heritage from the Lord, children a reward from him." Dear Lord, today I am committing that I will pray for and cover my children in prayer every day, and I will talk with my children every day. I understand and recognize that my voice of wisdom, guidance, correction and blessing is the first voice that my children will hear. Therefore, I am asking for help as I navigate leading and stewarding the gift of children that You have graciously entrusted to me. Help me, Lord, to recognize the gifts that You have given to my children and direct me in the path of sharpening them as arrows so that You can use them for your glory. In Jesus' name. Amen.

WHEN YOU PRAY

Today, all of Heaven stands at attention to hear the cries of my

Heart._____

_____

_____

_____

_____

_____

_____

_____

_____

_____

_____

_____

_____

_____

_____

_____

ABOUT THE AUTHOR

Matthew K Thompson is a loving husband, caring father to his two children Tyveshe and Matthew Jr., a devoted grandfather, a charismatic leader, avid sports lover, author, worshipper and senior pastor of Jubilee Christian Church.

Matthew has exhibited a desire and determination to advance the kingdom of God. Growing up as a preacher's son, Matthew witnessed the great impact of many influential leaders in the community. After graduating from Morehouse College, his purposeful journey in ministry began in 1996. In 2010, Matthew became the senior pastor of Jubilee Christian Church and in 2014 he formally succeeded his father.

Matthew and his wife, Mona Thompson, lead a multi-generational, 7,000-member church in the New England area. Together they cultivate an atmosphere that empowers and champions individuals to reach their potential and fulfill their purpose.

In 2018 Matthew was named in Boston Magazine's 100 Most Influential People in Boston. The article identified him as one of the leaders/influencers being watched who are truly shaping the city.

Matthew K. Thompson has recently released his second book titled, When You Pray, accompanied by his first prayer album. This book, along with the guiding activities within, moves readers into the understanding that no matter our position in life we are to focus on the main thing: time spent with the Father and coming to know Him intimately.

Stay connected with Pastor Matthew on all social media platforms with the handle @pmktjubilee or visit www.matthewkthompson.com